2016

Computer Security for the everyday user

Michael Magara MSIA, CISSP

5/10/2016

Everyday Computer Security

This course of instruction is designed not only for the computer user while using a company computer but can be applied to the average computer end-use while using their personal computing devices at home.

It goes without saying that 2015 was the year of the hacker. One only needed to watch the morning or evening news to see one security breach after another. All of the effecting corporate America and the data these companies collect, maintain, and use every day in the performance of their business. Therefore, this course is designed to provide guidance and standard security practices that the average individual can employ to better protect the computer systems they use at home and work from becoming the victim of a hacking attempt.

Contents

Workstation / Computer Security

In recent years we have found that in corporate environment workstation security is being managed by the company's IT department (Network Administration Staff) through the use of Group Policies applied in the Microsoft Domain environments. From and administrative perspective this entails the IT department applying policies that are to be consistent throughout the corporate network. Companies will apply.

- ➢ Windows updates.
- ➢ Anti-virus software and updates.
- ➢ Standardized Email infrastructure.
- ➢ Standardized desktop environment.
- ➢ Standardized application environments.
- ➢ Standardized security setting such as log-ins.

By applying these standards, the company attempts to limit their attack surface and make it harder for the hacker to compromise or better known as defense in depth. Let us take a brief look at each of the policies that corporate networks implement.

One of the major issues is that the everyday computer user must implement all of these policies by themselves and for themselves while knowing little about computer security and what they should be trying to configure on their computer.

During your reading I will attempt to provide you with a basic knowledge of computer security while making some recommendations on how to use your computer system more securely.

Windows Updates

With previous versions of the operating system (Microsoft) updates, hot-fixes, patches, and service packs were published by Microsoft every Tuesday of the week. This was known as Up-Date Tuesday and relied on the IT staff to download the updates from the Microsoft Web Site. Filter out updates that did not apply to the environments they managed. Then test those updates that did apply in an effort to ensure that any applied up-date did not break the operating system, the applications running on the operating system, or network communications.

As some of you might remember prior to Windows 7 these updates were downloaded to the user's workstation and advertised to allow them to install the updates as time permitted. Starting with Windows 7 these updates were downloaded to the user's computer. Cached until the user selected system shutdown and then the up-dates were installed for the user. This process has also been ported into the Windows 10 operating system versions. Where the updates are pushed out by the corporate IT department and often installed with no user interaction or notice. This is especially helpful for the IT department and end-user because they can install updates without hindering the user's productivity as shown in the following example.

 Settings

 ADVANCED OPTIONS

Choose how updates are installed

| Automatic (recommended) ⌄ |

Keep everything running smoothly. We'll restart your device automatically when you're not using it. Updates won't download over a metered connection (where charges may apply).

 Give me updates for other Microsoft products when I update Windows.

View your update history

Choose how updates are delivered

Activity:

In this activity the student learns how to manage updates in a Microsoft Windows 10 environment and then in a Microsoft Windows 7 environment.

Windows 10

1. Click in the search bar located in the lower left corner of the desktop

2.

3. Type **Windows Update**
4. Select Windows Update settings from the menu and it will open the following

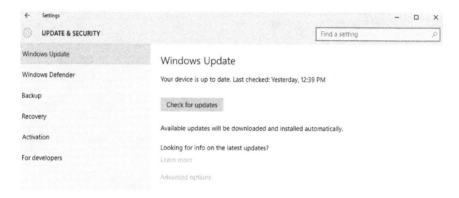

5. Left Click (Check for updates)

The Windows update program will make a connection to Microsoft over the internet and check to ensure that any updates available for your system are identified, downloaded, and made available for the user to install into their computer system as shown in the following screen capture.

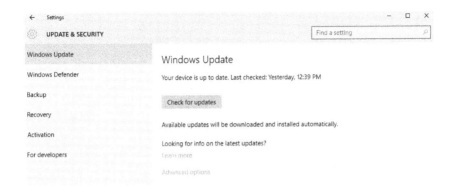

From the settings panel the end-user can

a. Have the operating system check for updates and install any updates found

Windows Defender

Windows defender is an anti-malware application built into and maintained by Microsoft to assist the user with ensuring that they do not become compromised by a virus, worm, or other form of malicious code that could delete, modify, or otherwise harm their computer system. The program provides real-time protection to the computer user that assists the user by scanning and keeping malicious code from installing on the computer as shown in the following screen capture. Microsoft provides updates to Defender to ensure that it contains the signatures for all the latest forms of malware that a user could encounter while using their computer today.

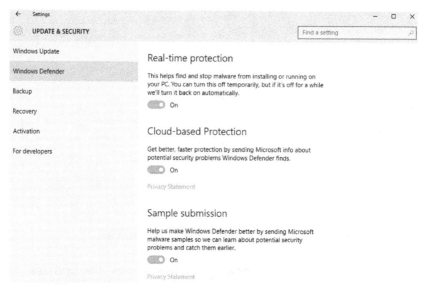

The user can also perform a scan of their computer system using Windows Defender by following the steps in Activity 2 below.

Activity 2 – Windows Defender

1. Left click in the search dialog box in the lower left corner of the screen.

2. Type Windows Defender and press the enter key

3. Select the type of scan they wish to perform (Quick, Full, or Custom). For our exercise we will perform a quick scan of our computers by selecting Quick from our choices and then left clicking on the Scan now button.

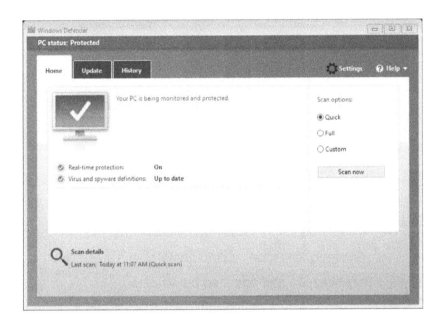

As the Windows Defender is scanning the computer system the user can continue with other tasks that they might need to work on as Defender will run in background and requires no further user interaction.

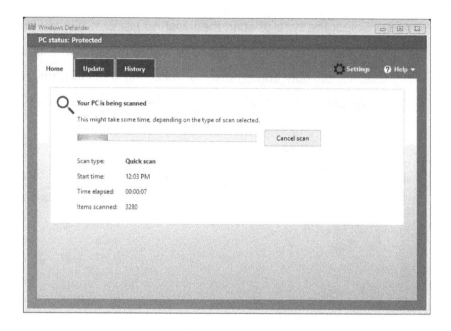

4. Once the scan has completed (as shown below) Windows Defender will indicate to the user whether or not the scan had detected any issues.

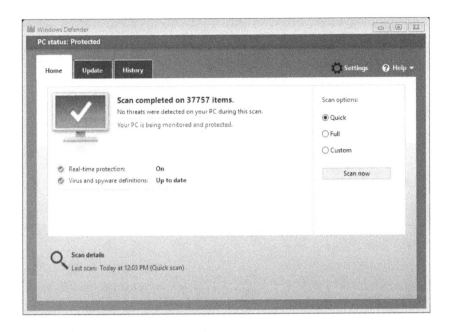

If Defender detected any issues the user can left, click the History tab and click on the view details button to see what Defender was able to identify as shown below.

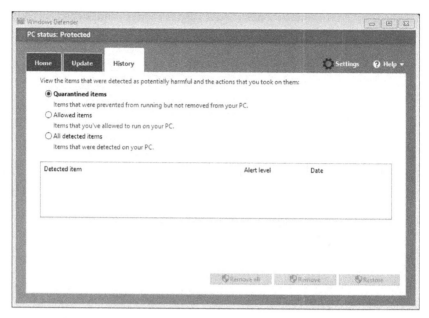

If any items are displayed the user can remove all the items from their computer system, remove individual items, or restore items that they know are of no harm to the computer system.

Windows Backup

One of the items a pc technician always runs into and always asks before working on some end-users, clients, or friend's pc is "do you have all your data backed up?". The typical answer from the home end-user is no. From the corporate worker the typical answer is also no or the IT people take care of that for us. As you can see in the screen capture Windows 10 comes with a back-up program installed that allows the user to back-up their files to another drive. The other drive can and most often is a USB drive that the user has purchased.

For home users it is recommended that the user back-up their files no less than monthly but preferably weekly. This will allow the user to recover any files that have been accidentally deleted, lost, or destroyed when the computer crashes.

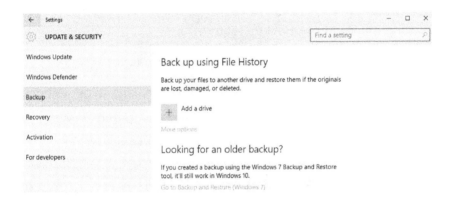

As mentioned earlier if the corporate environment the IT Administrative staff will normally redirect the user's documents folder to a shared network drive where everything is backed-up on a regular basis. Thus the corporate user does not have to back-up their work station while at work.

One of the interesting aspects of the corporate IT Administrative staff redirecting and backing-up the user's documents folders is this only works when the user is connected to the network. If the user is using some type of mobile device i.e. laptop, tablet, or iPad then the data on their devices are not normally backed-up. Thus the end-user's data becomes vulnerable to loss, corruption, or deletion.

Activity 3 Windows Backup

In this activity the user will perform a backup of their data using the Windows Backup feature.

1. In the search dialog box located in the lower left corner of the screen left click in the box and type Windows Backup. The menu will display Backup and Restore. Left click the Backup and Restore menu selection.

2.

3. Left click Set Backup as shown below

Control Panel Home

Create a system image

Create a system repair disc

Back up or restore your files

Backup

Windows Backup has not been set up.   Set up backup

Restore

Windows could not find a backup for this computer.

Select another backup to restore files from

The system will start the backup program which will allow you to back up your data.

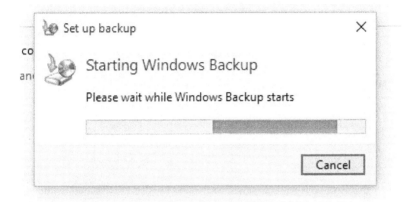

As shown in the screen capture below you can then select the location where you would like to back up your data to.

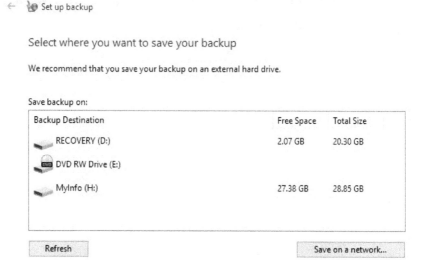

At this time, you can back up your data to your recovery drive, a DVD drive, or a USB drive as shown above called MyInfo (H).

This process will create a system image that you can restore from when your computer fails.

Other Backup Methods

One of the most popular methods for backing up your data today is the cloud. Cloud storage is really a matter to taking your information. Documents, Pictures, and other information that you do not want to loose and copying the information to a public cloud (internet) storage location.

There are many choices for the computer user when selecting cloud storage. Some of the choices are Microsoft OneDrive, Drobox, Google Drive, and others. With the use of Microsoft Windows 10 the average user has 53 Gigabytes worth of storage that they can access on the Microsoft Cloud for my favorite word FREE. Along with the Microsoft Windows 10 operating system giving the user access to free cloud storage the Microsoft Office program also gives the user access to the same cloud storage.

Accessing OneDrive is as simple as

Activity 3.1 Accessing OneDrive

1. The first step in accessing your one drive is to press the Windows key on your keyboard shown below. Then start typing OneDrive. The OneDrive application will be the first item in the menu list on the left side of the computer screen.

To save a doc you're working on to OneDrive, select a OneDrive folder from the list of save locations. To move files to OneDrive, open File Explorer and then drag them into a OneDrive folder.

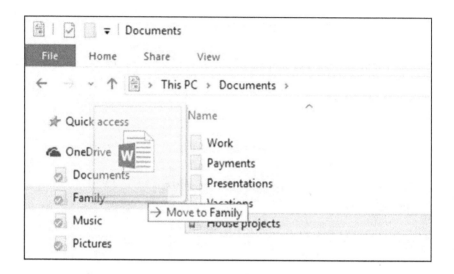

User Passwords

No discussion on computer security would ever be complete without at least discussing user passwords and how to create a secure password that is difficult for the hacker to obtain. The hacker can obtain a users' password by guessing the password, or trying to attack the password its self with a wide array of tools at their disposal. Therefore, it is important for the user to create a password that would be difficult for the attacker to guess and difficult for the tools the attacker will use to break.

Creating a secure password is a rather easy process for the user. A recommendation from the security industry world-wide is to create a password that contains at least one uppercase letter, one lowercase letter, a number, a symbol, and be between seven and ten characters in length. This type of password would look something like the following examples.

1. M1K3mag
2. P@ssw0rd
3. Pa$$w0rd

By Creating a password in a similar fashion as those above the attacker will have a more difficult time trying to guess the password.

We are not quite done yet with passwords. Once you have the secure password you must change it once in a while. I know we went through all the trouble of creating a secure password and now he is telling me I have to change it. What's up with that? Well without getting into a lot of high end technology jargon the issue is that the older the password is the more of a chance the attacker has to break the password and gain access to the system. This does not mean that you have to change your password every week but you should change your password every 45 to 90 days. This ensures that if the attacker has obtained the encrypted copy of your password it is only going to be of use to them for a short period of time.

The Internet and Internet Browsers

Our first discussion in this section is the deals with the internet, what it is, and how to use it safely. One of the primary tools that an attacker will use to compromise (hack into) a computer system whether it be a personal computer or company computer is the internet. Hackers will create attractive looking web sites that attempt to lure the un-expecting user to visit their site. They will also create fake websites that to the average user appear to be the original site as shown in our example of a fake Facebook sign-in page shown below.

Retrieved from http://fb-awesome-tricks.blogspot.com/2013/12/how-to-hackers-hack-facebook-account.html

If you examine the URL closely this page redirects you to https://www.*facelook*.com/fakepage.html. Once the user is presented this page and enters their user name and password the hacker can then take over their Facebook page by capturing their user log-on name and password. After capturing the user name and password the attacker could then attempt to use those credentials in an attempt to log on to other web-sites. This type of an attack is commonly referred to as a Phishing Attack. In a phishing attack the attacker attempts to gather user information that could be used to log-on to web-sites pretending to be the legitimate user.

In another example of how the hacker could use the internet to hack into someone's computer the attacker creates a fake web site advertisement such as the one shown below.

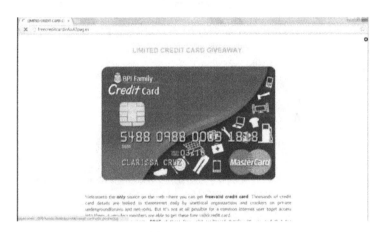

Retrieved from https://www.youtube.com/watch?v=8Wwahtpiwkw

Using this method, the attacker temps the un-suspecting user into thinking that they can get a free credit card by simply filling out an application form. Once the user fills out the application form the hacker has enough of their information to perform identity theft and apply for any number of credit card using the victim's information.

Another example that often has success is to trick the user into thinking that there is something wrong with their computer. The attacker will display a page to the user telling them that they have a virus or other malicious code on their computer and for a (blank) dollar amount they will install software that will remove the malicious code or repair their computer for them as shown below.

Retrieved from https://malwaretips.com/blogs/cpuwarning-com-virus/

The most effective methodology the hacker can use to compromise the user's computer, bank accounts, and personal information is to just trick the unsuspecting user into clicking on something that will compromise their computer.

To prevent yourself from falling victim to these type of attacks you can apply a few simple rules.

1. If it seems too good to be true it is.
2. Never click a hyperlink sent to you via email or instant messaging if you do not know who sent it to you.
3. Before clicking on a hyperlink and filling out any personal information look at the URL. Is the URL from the company that is requesting information? If you are unsure if the URL is legitimate call the company and ask them. They will be more than happy to assist you.

Browsers used in searching the Web as reported by the W3C (World Wide Web Consortium) in December of 2015 show

2015	Chrome	IE	Firefox	Safari	Opera
December	68.0 %	6.3 %	19.1 %	3.7 %	1.5 %
November	67.4 %	6.8 %	19.2 %	3.9 %	1.5 %
October	66.5 %	6.9 %	20.0 %	3.8 %	1.4 %

Most organizations will support one or two different internet browsers within the company network. These two browsers are most likely Internet Explorer (Edge) or Google Chrome. As shown above according to the W3C the most popular internet browser (regardless of what Microsoft thinks) is Google Chrome.

For the purpose of this discussion we will start with what from my experience most corporations utilize with in their corporate environment Internet Explorer. Early this year Microsoft had announced that it is stopping all support for Internet Explorer versions 7, 8, 9, and 10. This leaves the computer user Internet Explorer 11 and Edge. Internet Explorer 11 is built into Windows 10 and the user can upgrade to Internet Explorer 11 in Windows 8 and Windows 8.1. The interface is the familiar Internet Explorer interface with few changes in appearance as shown below.

Internet Explores still has security settings that allow the end-user to customize the application for their purpose such as trusted sites, in-private browsing, and favorites. The trusted sites feature allows the user to add sites to the Internet Explorer settings of different sites that they visit that the user knows are safe and has a medium security setting as shown below.

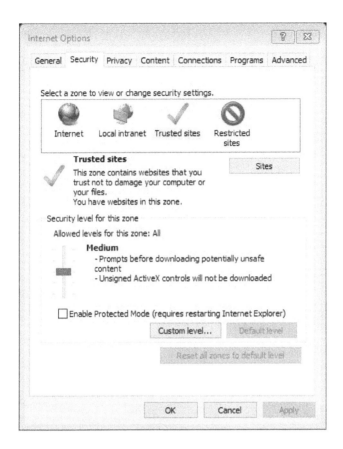

The trusted sites category with a medium setting for security prompts the user before the system will download unsafe content and is the recommended setting for most end-users. The internet options also contain settings for the internet which as a security setting of medium-high. At this setting the user is provided protection by Internet Explorer and is the recommended setting for internet browsing. The setting will prompt the user before downloading potentially unsafe content, as well as unsigned ActiveX controls.

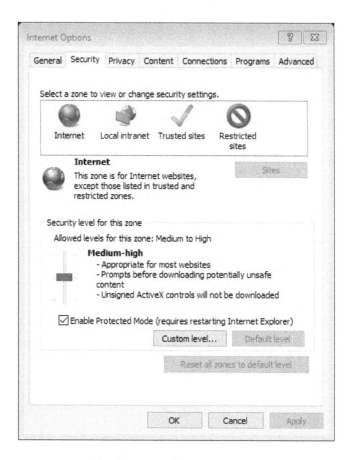

Internet Explorer also has settings for site that the user deems unsafe or that they do not wish anyone who uses the computer to visit. These settings are referred to as restricted sites. Once the user enters a sight into the restricted sites category (shown below).

When the user attempts to visit the site the maximum amount of security settings are applied to the site in an attempt to keep the user's computer safe from harmful content and the high security settings are applied to Internet Explorer.

Some interesting facts on how the average user uses the internet are provided below.

US users do 129 searches per month
http://www.comscore.com/Insights...

Google users in the US do 37.9 searches per month
Nielsen Online Announces December U.S. Search Share Rankings

Bing users do 5 searches per day.

Google users do 5.6 searches per day

Yahoo! users do 7.8 searches per day.

September Search Share: The Bing train keeps rolling but not at Google's expense

Mobile users do 1.1 searches per day

Android users do 2.65 searches per day

So what do these facts have to do with computer security? Not getting infected with malware? And using the computer securely (or avoid being hacked into). The answer is quite simple the average attacker will create fake websites as well as fake advertisements in an effort to get you to compromise your own computer by clicking on a hyperlink to one of these malicious sites. It is much easier to have the user compromise their own computer rather than hack into the computer system.

So how do we protect against these fake web sites and advertisements that the hacker places on the web? One way we can prevent this type of compromise is with the internet browser that we are using. The developers of the browsers have added the functionality to screen sites that have been reported as being unsafe. When every you see a message on the screen that the site is unsafe do not go to the site. One of the other ways we can protect our systems is by running a good anti-virus software program. While the third is by examining the URL to see where it is going to take us. If it does not look legitimate most likely it is not and we should close that page.

Antivirus

Everyone knows about or is aware of antivirus software (which I will call antimalware software) and everyone has their opinion on which one is the best. Therefore, I am not going to try and convince you to change your mind and use one that I recommend. However, there are some basic steps that we must perform regardless of which product we use.

The first is to choose and use an antimalware software package. We must keep it up to date (Daily), and we must monitor its functionality. Without running an antimalware program on the computer the user's computer is bound to become infected with one form or another of malware. Yet to this day whenever I repair a user's computer this is still one of the biggest issues that I find. The user is either running an outdated software package, the virus definitions are out dated, or they are not running antimalware protection at all.

By maintaining the antimalware program, the program is routinely going to the internet manufactures web site to download new definitions. These definitions allow the program to identify new threats and protect the computer from those threats. If the user does not ensure that new definitions are downloaded and installed the program cannot protect the computer from the new threats that are introduced every day.

According to Virginia Harrison and Joes Pagliery from CNN Money nearly one million new malware threats released every day. While reportedly more than 317 million new threats were introduced in 2015. These figures are alarming and if the everyday user fails to protect their computer systems from these types of threats everyday they are sure to be compromised.

Email

While most users are becoming more and more computer savvy concerning email we continually hear every day of another attack connected to the user and their use of email. Of course we have a wide variety of email clients that people use from Gmail, Yahoo mail, Microsoft Outlook, and etc. One of the key ingredients is that email is being used by the bad guy to gather information, hack into computer systems, perform identity theft, and perform extortion.

Let's start by examination of extortion via email. One of the most popular way the attacker is using this process is by sending the unsuspecting user an email offering them something, attaching a fake invoice or including a malicious hyperlink. Once the user interacts with the email by clicking on something (anything) the attackers malicious code executes. The code then encrypts data on the users machine and displays a page the tells the user if they do not pay a certain dollar amount the encrypted data on their computer would be deleted as shown in the following screen captures from an article written by Eric Geier from PCWorld on 13 January of 2014.

Retrieved from http://www.pcworld.com/article/2084002/how-to-rescue-your-pc-from-ransomware.html

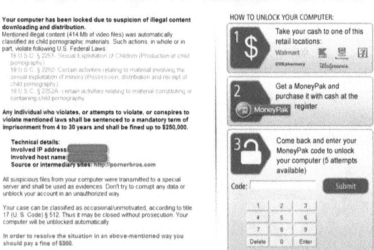

Permanent lock on 05/01/2013 5:20 p.m. EST

Retrieved from http://www.pcworld.com/article/2084002/how-to-rescue-your-pc-from-
ransomware.html

So the question is how do we as everyday users prevent becoming a victim of these type of attacks and the answer is quite simple. First of all, ensure that we have antimalware software installed, running, and up to date on our computer systems. Secondly do not open emails, or click on hyperlinks, or open attachments unless we know what they are and they have been scanned for malicious code!

An additional concern with email is when the attacker does not compromise your computer but attempts to have the user provide them with all of their personal information, date of birth, social security number, address, credit card numbers, etc. This is referred to as social engineering and there are many forms of this type of an attack. I will not attempt to make you an expert in social engineering attacks but we need to be aware that they exist and not respond to them. One such attack is shown in an email that I received not too long ago and is shown below.

M. A. GONZALO
Executive Director/ Financial Controller
Repsol Petroleum Corporation, Madrid.

Dear Sir/Ma,

I am the financial controller of Repsol Petroleum Company - Madrid, Spain. I and my colleagues are in charge of offshore remittance in this Corporation (Repsol Petroleum). We are seeking your assistance to transfer the sum of Thirty Eight Million (US$38,000,000.00) to your account for further private investment. This amount accrued from an over-invoiced contract amount for the construction of an Oil Refinery Sub- stations in 2013 to expatriate companies. The contract was originally valued for One Hundred and Twenty Seven Million United States Dollar US$127,000,000.00) but we manipulated the figure to read One Hundred and Sixty Five Million United States Dollars($165,000,000.00). We want to transfer the extra $38,000,000.00 to your bank account.

This contract has been completely executed and the original contractors have been paid all their contract bills less this $38,000,000.00 through Banco Santander Madrid Spain. We shall forward your name to the Bank for the payment of the balance US$38Million. Be rest assured that all modalities are set for smooth execution of this viable transaction. For your assistance, we have agreed to remunerate you with 30% because it is impossible for us to claim the amount here in Spain without foreign collaboration. 3% has been mapped out for any miscellaneous expenses incurred by either party during this business, and 67% for my colleagues and myself.

This explains exactly why we will make a concrete agreement between you and us, should you be willing to assist in this deal. All modalities to effect the payment and subsequent transfer of this money have been worked out. This transaction is 100% risk free but requires 100 percent confidentiality. You must do this transaction alone! This is a golden opportunity which you must not afford to miss. We chose you for this transaction because we believe that good friends can be discovered and businesses such as this cannot be realized without trust. You can be rest assured that absolute security is guaranteed, and realistic success is 100% certain.

I await your urgent response.

Best Regards,

M. A. GONZALO

Reply Reply All Forward IM

Tue 1/26/2016 1:32 AM

M. A. GONZALO <tettelbachm1@lasalle.edu>

Repsol Company !!!

To

M. A. GONZALO
Executive Director/ Financial Controller
Repsol Petroleum Corporation, Madrid.

If we examine the email just briefly we see the email address of tettelbachm1@lasalle.edu. The last part of the email

(.edu) signifies that the email came from an educational institution, or at least that is what they want us to think. Then if we look at the first part of the email address we see (tettelbachm1) but the person sending the email is a M.A. Gonzalo. Another interesting part of the email is this individual is supposedly from Madrid Spain. Now why would them be contacting me? If you read the email it sounds too good to be true. Wait what is the old saying if it sounds too good to be true it probably is. Well this is just one example of different types of techniques that the malicious individual could use to obtain money from the unsuspecting individual.

Ok so what is our protection from these type of attacks.

1. If you do not know what is in the attachment do not open it.
2. If you do not know who sent you the email be extremely careful and do not open it.
3. Do not respond to unsolicited emails.
4. Do not give out your personal information before calling the company first.
5. Ask a friend

Software

No conversation on computer security would be even close to complete if we did not include a discussion on software that is available to the average computer user. In the computer world we have a lot of different choices for computer software.

These software programs fall roughly into one of three different categories. Licensed software products, Shareware software, and Freeware. So let's examine these three categories.

Licensed software is designed and created to allow us to perform different types of activities on our computer systems. The companies that create the software have in place all sorts of different procedures in place to ensure that the software works correctly on our computers. The software undergoes a complete check to ensure that it does not contain malicious code that could harm or make our computers vulnerable to some type of attack.

Freeware software is just that software that is made available to the general public to download and install on their computer systems for Free. Examples of freeware would be programs such as Adobe Acrobat Reader. Adobe created this program to allow the typical user the ability to read pdf documents on their computer without having to purchase and install the full Adobe program. Therefore, using Adobe Acrobat Reader as our example. A legitimate company created the program, tested the program, and then published the program for use by the general public. This would indicate that the program would be free of viruses, worms, and other malware.

Shareware software is a software program that originally provided to the user for free. The user can make copies of the program and distribute the program on their own. The shareware version of the software is offered for free but often with reduced functionality. To obtain full functionality the user is required to purchase a license for the program.

Ok so we have three different types of software available on the internet for our use. So the question now becomes how does this affect the security of our computer systems. The answer lies in where is the user downloading the software from. Are they downloading it from the manufactures web site or a site the specializes in illegal (unlicensed) copies of the software. One the user decides to obtain the software from one of these sites they are subject to downloading the software they wanted but the software would have been modified by the poster with some type of malware. This malware will often be some type of keystroke logger or tracking software that captures every keystroke the user enters on their computer and then sends that information to the hacker. Imagine a software package that is capturing every keystroke you make on your computer. What would it capture? How many different user names and passwords would it capture? Would it include your user name and password for your on-line banking as well as others?

So what is my point? Before downloading ANY type of software make sure you know where you are downloading it from and what you are really downloading to your computer. Do not download software from sites other than the manufactures site. Do not download software that should be licensed from sites that offer a cracked version of the software. A cracked version is one that someone has figured out a way to bypass the license requirements for the software package. Doing so not only is against the law but is a sure way to download an infected version of the software package.

Conclusion

While computer security is a complete field of study in the information technology industry and can take many months if not years of study. The average computer user can increase their odds of not being hacked into, infected with malware, and not lose their data by simply applying some basic computer security steps as outlined in this book. A very smart man that I know and respect once told me that the average user just makes some simple mistakes while using their computer. If we all would just think a little more before we clicked on something, opened an attachment, or downloaded that free software we would all be much better off.